Bass Eat Their Own Young!

Miriam Coleman

PowerKiDS
press™
New York

Published in 2014 by The Rosen Publishing Group, Inc.
29 East 21st Street, New York, NY 10010

First Edition

Editor: Joanne Randolph
Book Design: Kate Vlachos
Photo Research: Katie Stryker

Photo Credits: Cover Steve Maslowski/Photo Researchers/Getty Images; front cover (series title) © iStockphoto/lishenjun; back cover graphic -Albachiaraa-/Shutterstock.com; p. 5 StevenRussellSmithPhotos/Shuttertstock.com; p. 6 DEA/C. Galasso/De Agostini Picture Library/Getty Images; p. 7 (left) Vstock LLC/Getty Images; p. 7 (right) Pete Niesen/Shutterstock.com; p. 8 Vera Kalyuzhnaya/Shutterstock.com; p. 9 Shaun Lowe/E+/Getty Images; pp. 10, 22 George Grall/National Geographic/Getty Images; pp. 11, 14, 16–17, 21 iStockphoto/Thinkstock; pp. 12–13 Gary Meszaros/Photo Researchers/Getty Images; p. 15 Tom McHugh/Photo Researchers/Getty Images; pp. 18, 19 © Michelson, Robert S/Animals Animals; p. 20 Martin Shields/Photo Researchers/Getty Images.

Library of Congress Cataloging-in-Publication Data

Coleman, Miriam, author.
 Bass eat their own young! / by Miriam Coleman. — First edition.
     pages cm. — (Disgusting animal dinners)
 Includes index.
 ISBN 978-1-4777-2887-1 (library) — ISBN 978-1-4777-2974-8 (pbk.) —
 ISBN 978-1-4777-3046-1 (6-pack)
 1. Basses (Fish)—Behavior—Juvenile literature. 2. Basses (Fish)—Juvenile literature. I. Title.
 QL637.9.P46C65 2014
 597.73—dc23
                                        2013024483

Manufactured in the United States of America

CPSIA Compliance Information: Batch #W14PK6: For Further Information contact Rosen Publishing, New York, New York at 1-800-237-9932

CONTENTS

Meet the Bass

Bass are a favorite fish for people who love to go fishing for sport. These large, active creatures provide a fun challenge to try to catch. They also offer up a lot of flesh that people like to eat.

Although bass have few predators underwater, people aren't the only ones enjoying a dinner of tasty bass. Bass often eat other bass! They don't just eat strangers, either. Bass often eat their family members, including their brothers and sisters and even their own babies.

This largemouth bass is leaping from the water trying to throw off a fisherman's line.

Two Families of Bass

Largemouth bass are black bass and make their home in freshwater.

Two different families of fish go by the name bass. They are not related to each other. One family, called the sunfish, is made up of freshwater fish that live in North American lakes and rivers. Six **species** of sunfish that are larger and longer than the rest are called black bass. Black bass include largemouth bass and smallmouth bass.

The other family of bass is called the sea bass. This family includes the giant sea bass and the common bass. The two families of bass have a few things in common. They are all large fish, with spiny fins. They are all skilled and hungry hunters that prey on smaller fish and other sea creatures.

Left: The spotted bass is another kind of black bass. It has a smaller mouth than the other two species.
Below: The giant potato cod, or potato bass, is a kind of sea bass. Some kinds of sea bass, including the potato cod, have been fished so much they are in danger of becoming extinct.

Where Do Bass Live?

Although there are a few freshwater fish in the sea bass family, most of them live in **tropical** or **temperate marine habitats** all over the world. The common bass is often found around the coasts of Britain, and the stone bass is found all over the Atlantic Ocean and the Mediterranean Sea.

Black bass live in freshwater ponds and lakes.

Striped bass are bass that migrate between salt water and freshwater. They live in the ocean but travel to freshwater to lay their eggs.

Black bass are native to the eastern United States. Because people love to fish for them so much, they have been **introduced** to other places as well. These fish can now be found all over North America and as far away as Japan and Europe.

Largemouth Bass

Largemouth bass are big fish that can grow to be more than 2 feet (61 cm) long and weigh more than 20 pounds (9 kg). They have powerful jaws on mouths that reach back out beyond their eyes.

As you can see from these pictures below and at right, largemouth bass got their name for a reason. Their mouths can open up quite wide to catch larger prey.

They are usually dark green, with yellowish-green sides and a dark **horizontal** stripe down the middle of each side. They have spines on their front fins, and their dorsal, or back, fins have two parts.

Largemouth bass live in lakes, slow-moving streams, ponds, and rivers. They eat mostly smaller fish and also enjoy frogs, shellfish, and insects. They hunt for food near plants that grow in and around the water, such as lily pads and weeds.

Disgusting Bass Facts!

1 Common bass have fins with sharp spines that can pierce human flesh.

2 Largemouth bass can eat prey up to half their own length in size.

3 Largemouth bass usually eat other fish headfirst.

4 Common bass have teeth on every surface of their mouths, even their tongues.

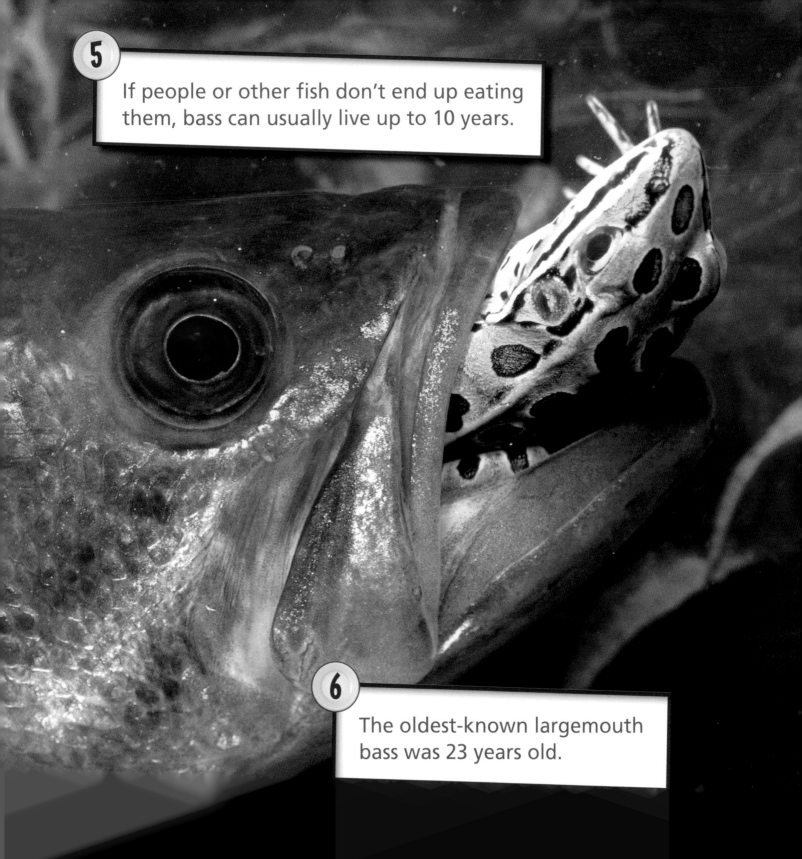

5 If people or other fish don't end up eating them, bass can usually live up to 10 years.

6 The oldest-known largemouth bass was 23 years old.

Smallmouth Bass

Smallmouth bass are close relatives of largemouth bass. They are usually green or bronze, with several dark vertical stripes down the sides of their bodies. Although they are also big fish and can grow to be more than 7.5 pounds (3 kg), smallmouth bass do not reach the same sizes as largemouth bass.

It is easy to see here that the smallmouth bass's mouth ends before its eye, which is one way it differs from largemouth bass.

Just like largemouth bass, smallmouth bass are popular sport fish. That means people like to try to catch them.

Their dorsal fins contain between 13 and 15 soft rays, and they have spines on their backs.

Smallmouth bass prefer to live in large lakes with clear water, as well as cool streams that have swiftly flowing water and gravel at the bottom. They eat mostly minnows and small suckerfish and crayfish in the fall.

Building a Nest

In the summertime, when black bass are ready to have babies, the male builds a nest on the floor of a lake or riverbed. Using his fins, the male bass makes a large circle by digging up gravel, shells, and plant roots.

When the nest is ready, the female swims up and lays her eggs. She can lay between 2,000 and 40,000 eggs. The young bass will hatch from the eggs in about a week. They will stay in the nest to feed and grow for another week.

The male and female bass come together and swim in certain patterns to get ready for the female to lay her eggs.

Guarding the Young

Right after **spawning**, the female bass leaves the nest. The male bass stays behind to protect the eggs and newly hatched young fish from harm. Young fish are called fry. When they are very young, they eat mostly **plankton** and tiny **crustaceans**. As they get a little bigger, they move on to insect larvae.

Here a smallmouth bass male is watching over the newly hatched. All those black specks are baby bass!

These are bass eggs in a rock nest. The father guards the eggs so that other animals do not eat them.

The father fights off predators, such as larger minnows and groups of other sunfish, that come to eat the fry. Sometimes one sunfish will draw the father away from the nest so that a larger group can attack the unguarded nest. The father bass must stay alert to protect his young.

Watch Out, Baby Bass!

Baby bass soon learn of another threat: their own parents! Female bass are very tired after spawning. They don't have much energy to hunt for food, and so they eat what is nearest and easiest. This is often their own young.

This is a young smallmouth bass. Small bass are an easy meal for many pond animals.

A heron has caught a young largemouth bass.

If they don't get eaten, young bass stay in the nest for about a week after they hatch. During the following few weeks, the young may leave the nest. They all stay together in a school called a brood swarm, though, which the father guards and protects. After three to four weeks, the young fish are ready to leave the nest alone. Now that they are no longer under his watch, the father sees his own young as just any other delicious prey.

Fish Cannibals

Bass are not the only fish that eat members of their own species. In fact, **cannibalism** is common among many kinds of fish. Although it seems disgusting to people, bass are not even alone in eating their own young. Fish hatch so many babies at a time that it can be hard to keep track of which ones belong to which parents.

Bass are active, hungry fish that are always on the move and looking for something to eat. The same qualities that drive bass to eat their own young make these creatures a favorite of people who love sportfishing.

Right now this bass male is guarding his fry. Soon, though, the urge to eat will become stronger than his drive to keep them safe.

GLOSSARY

cannibalism (KA-nuh-buh-liz-um) When animals eat their own kind.

crustaceans (krus-TAY-shunz) Animals that have no backbones and have hard shells and limbs and live mostly in water.

habitats (HA-beh-tats) The surroundings where animals or plants naturally live.

horizontal (hor-ih-ZON-til) Going from side to side.

introduced (in-truh-DOOSD) Brought into use, knowledge, or notice.

marine (muh-REEN) Having to do with the sea.

plankton (PLANK-ten) Plants and animals that drift with water currents.

spawning (SPAWN-ing) Releasing or depositing eggs.

species (SPEE-sheez) A single kind of living thing. All people are one species.

temperate (TEM-puh-rut) Not too hot or too cold.

tropical (TRAH-puh-kul) Having to do with the warm parts of Earth that are near the equator.

INDEX

WEBSITES

Due to the changing nature of Internet links, PowerKids Press has developed an online list of websites related to the subject of this book. This site is updated regularly. Please use this link to access the list: www.powerkidslinks.com/dad/bass/